Writing for Freedom

Writing for Freedom

A Story about Lydia Maria Child

by Erica Stux
illustrations by Mary O'Keefe Young

A Creative Minds Biography

Carolrhoda Books, Inc./Minneapolis

Carolrhoda Books, Inc.
A division of Lerner Publishing Group
241 First Avenue North
Minneapolis, MN 55401 U.S.A.

Website address: www.lernerbooks.com

Library of Congress Cataloging-in-Publication Data

Stux, Erica.
    Writing for freedom: a story about Lydia Maria Child / by Erica Stux ;
illustrated by Mary O'Keefe Young.
        p.   cm. — (A creative minds biography)
    Includes bibliographical references (p.) and index.
    Summary: A biography of the woman who risked her success in the
male-dominated literary world of nineteenth-century America to become a
passionate advocate for the abolition of slavery.
    ISBN 1-57505-439-6 (lib. bdg. : alk. paper)
    1. Child, Lydia Maria Francis, 1802–1880—Juvenile literature. 2. Women
authors, American—19th century—Biography—Juvenile literature.
3. Abolitionists—United States—Biography—Juvenile literature. [1. Child,
Lydia Maria Francis, 1802–1880. 2. Authors, American. 3. Abolitionists.
4. Women—Biography.] I. Young, Mary O'Keefe, ill. II. Title. III. Series.
PS1293.Z5 S78   2001
818'.309—dc21   99-050950

Manufactured in the United States of America
1 2 3 4 5 6 – MA – 06 05 04 03 02 01

Table of Contents

1

An Unusual Girl

Lydia Francis ran to her house on the corner of Salem and Ashland Streets in Medford, Massachusetts. She had finished school for the day and, as usual, rushed through the house to her older brother Convers's room. She was eager to see what new books he had brought home from school. Convers always told her in detail about the books he was reading. Best of all, he let her read them for herself. Lydia didn't always understand everything she read. But she took so much pleasure in the words and ideas. Besides, she could always ask Convers to explain something, even if he teased her first.

Lydia and Convers sat among his pile of books and talked about what he had learned that day in school. Soon their father would call them away to help with the household chores. But until then, they entertained themselves with stories, plays, and poems.

Lydia Francis was born on February 11, 1802. Like other young girls in the early 1800s, she went to school in a private home. At Ma'am Betty's, she learned reading, writing, and simple arithmetic. But she probably learned more from talking to her brother Convers. He taught her to examine ideas from all sides, the old as well as the new. From him she gained a great love of books. Whenever she had a few minutes to herself, that time was spent with a book.

Lydia was the youngest of five Francis children. By the time Lydia was born, her mother, Susannah Francis, had become ill. She had little strength left to give love or encouragement to young Lydia. To Mrs. Francis, her youngest daughter seemed different than other girls. She was outspoken and stubborn, and she read so many books! Lydia was grateful for Convers and her oldest sister, Susannah. They gave her as much attention as they could spare. Still, with aunts and uncles frequently visiting the large Francis family, and all the household chores to be done, Lydia often felt ignored.

Lydia's father, Convers Francis, worked long hours in his bakery every day except Sunday. Each day he turned out bread and biscuits and muffins with delightful aromas. His famous "Medford Crackers" always sold well and helped to make his business successful. He liked to tell his children that the way to have a comfortable life was through hard work rather than education. He put them to work at an early age, weeding the garden, feeding the chickens, and helping in the kitchen.

Occasionally, Mr. Francis would tell his children stories about the Medford citizens who helped fight against slavery. Lydia did not experience slavery firsthand because it had been outlawed in Massachusetts. But businessmen from the Southern states often brought one or two slaves along when they traveled north on business trips. Sometimes Medford citizens helped hide a slave who hoped to escape from his or her owner. Then the Southern businessman would have to return home without his slave, and the slave would be free. As Lydia listened to her father's tales, she was filled with admiration.

By the time Lydia was nine, her mother had become very ill and rarely left her bed. Lydia's oldest sister Susannah ran the household, but a year later she married and moved away. That same year, Convers left home to attend Harvard University. The sadness that Lydia felt was overwhelming. Her two favorite people, the only ones who paid attention to her, were gone.

Mrs. Francis's health continued to decline. Mary, Lydia's other sister, took over many of the household chores. When Lydia was twelve years old, Mrs. Francis died of tuberculosis. Four months later, in September 1814, Mary was engaged to be married. Lydia felt as though everyone in the family had abandoned her. Faced with the prospect of being left with her father, Lydia refused to attend Mary's wedding.

After Mary left home, father and daughter adjusted to their new situation. But it wasn't easy. Along with books, letters from Convers became the highlight of Lydia's life. Through these letters, she continued to learn about the world from her brother. She also attended Miss Swan's Female Academy, but what she learned there did not interest her much. She still did most of her learning on her own.

Mr. Francis worried that Lydia was spending too much time alone reading. It was time for her to become a proper young lady. That summer he sat her down and explained that he was going to sell the bakery. He had decided that Lydia should go and live with her sister Mary in Maine. It would be better for her, he said, than living in Medford with an old man.

Besides, Mary was expecting her first baby soon and could use Lydia's help.

Lydia wondered what her life would be like with Mary. She felt sad leaving her life in Medford—even if it had become lonely. But she was eager for new adventures and the love-filled home that she hoped her sister might provide.

Lydia sorted through her belongings, deciding what to take to Maine. Her dolls would have to stay. She was thirteen years old—too old for dolls. She packed her clothing and her favorite books into the chest her father provided. On the day of her departure, Mr. Francis carried her chest to the stagecoach. Then he kissed his daughter good-bye, and the stagecoach rumbled off toward Maine.

To Be Independent!

Norridgewock, Maine, was a town of four hundred families. It had a church, a school, a mill, and—most important to Lydia—a library. Mary's husband, Warren Preston, was a lawyer. To Lydia's delight, he also served as the town's librarian.

The Prestons had a busy household and were happy to have Lydia's help. Lawyers from nearby towns often came to Norridgewock to argue their cases in the local court. The Prestons were among those who had lawyers boarding with them for weeks at a time. That meant extra cooking and cleaning had to be done. Apple and pumpkin pies had to be baked. Wild ducks and turkeys had to be roasted. Salmon from the Kennebec River had to be dried and salted. The household held a mixture of wonderful odors— of apple cider, leather, and hickory wood.

Working alongside her sister and sometimes a hired girl, Lydia picked up many tricks of housekeeping. She learned how to run a household and how to knit, quilt, and embroider. Lydia didn't mind the extra work. The visitors brought news from other towns, and the dining room was the scene of lively discussions.

At the Norridgewock school, Lydia studied French, German, and history. She wished she could learn Latin, Greek, and natural history, like Convers had when he was her age. But she knew why those subjects weren't taught in her school. Girls were supposed to be gentle, modest, and good-natured so that they would become good wives and mothers. Girls had no use for Latin or natural history, it was believed. While gentleness and modesty were good in real life, Lydia thought they made for dull reading. Luckily for her, she was allowed to have the run of the town's library.

In her weekly letters to Convers, Lydia wrote of her dissatisfaction with the girls' school. She also wrote about the authors she was reading. She especially liked the strong female characters in books by the Scottish author Sir Walter Scott. His popular historical novels captivated her imagination. She could picture herself being as daring as his characters.

Once Lydia formed opinions of certain authors, she clung to her views. When Convers wrote that she had misunderstood a famous poem by John Milton, she refused to agree. Fifteen-year-old Lydia responded to her Harvard-educated brother immediately. Whether the ideas she had formed were wrong or not, she wrote proudly, "they are entirely my own."

School, books, and chores kept Lydia busy. But sometimes, when she had time to herself, she took long walks to the edge of town. She liked the white birch trees and the sound of the wind in the aspens. Chickadees whistled their high-pitched notes to her as she walked. Often a wood thrush warbled its flutelike song from deep in the woods. She imagined that goblins lived in the pine woods where the trees grew so close together that sunlight never broke through.

Up the river and beyond the pine woods lay separate villages of Penobscot and Abenaki Indians. Always friendly and curious, Lydia tried talking to the Indian women. Though at first aloof, they soon responded to her offer of friendship.

The Indian people Lydia met showed her how they built their homes with birchbark walls. She learned how they made baskets out of reeds and how they decorated their deerskin clothing with beads. They also told her about the sad history of their people—how English settlers had taken away their land and killed many of their people. Their stories made Lydia angry. She hoped the Indian people would not have to suffer anymore.

Through her sister, the local Indians, and the books she read, Lydia was learning a lot. And for several years, life in Maine continued in the same pleasant way. But by the time she turned seventeen, she had begun to grow restless.

When Lydia finished her studies at the girls' school, she found a job as a teacher. Lydia enjoyed working in a local school and earning some money of her own. She wondered how it would feel to be truly independent.

Just after Lydia turned nineteen, she got the chance to find out. An offer had come to teach school in the nearby town of Gardiner. As much as Lydia enjoyed living with her sister, she looked forward to her life in Gardiner. She would be able to earn her own way and decide how to spend her free time.

Lydia could hardly wait to tell Convers the good

news. "I hope my dear brother," she wrote, "that you feel as happy as I do. Not that I have formed any high-flown expectations. All I expect is, that, if I am industrious and prudent I shall be *independent.*"

3

A New Name

Lydia had been teaching only a year when a special letter came from Convers. As Lydia read the letter, she grew more and more excited. Convers had moved to Watertown, Massachusetts, to become a minister. He was about to be married to Abby Bradford Allyn. Did Lydia want to come live with them?

Watertown, being close to Boston, was sure to be a more exciting place than Gardiner. Boston was becoming an important center of learning. Almost every evening a person could attend a public meeting or go to a lecture by someone wishing to share knowledge or opinions. Of course Lydia would come! She could always teach in Watertown if she wanted to.

When Lydia arrived in Watertown, she had her name changed from Lydia Francis to Lydia Maria Francis. She asked everyone to call her Maria. She wanted to have a new name to go along with her new life.

Maria's life in Watertown was even more fulfilling than she had expected. There were plenty of books in Convers's house, and interesting men and women often joined the family at the dinner table. Maria listened, her dark eyes fixed on each speaker, as the men talked. She asked questions and offered comments of her own. She was pleased when the guests took her remarks seriously.

The men around her brother's table often spoke about ways to improve society and make a difference in the world. What they said made a lot of sense to Maria. She wished she could accomplish something important. But what could a young lady of barely twenty do? All her reading seemed to tell her that women were not as good as men, mentally or physically.

One Sunday in early 1824, Maria came across a review of a long poem based on New England's history. The poem described a war between American Indians and English settlers in the early 1600s. The reviewer asked why more American writers did not make use of their country's history in their stories. It would be a fit subject for a work of fiction. Sir Walter Scott had written wonderful novels about Scotland's history. But few Americans had tried to write something similar.

Maria's imagination went to work immediately. Why not write a story about American history and American Indians? After all, she knew something about Abenaki and Penobscot Indians. And she was quite familiar with the historical novels of Sir Walter Scott.

That very day, she sat down at her desk and began to write. The first chapter of a story took shape as she scribbled on a sheet of paper. "I know not what impelled me," Maria recalled later. "I had never dreamed of such a thing as turning author." Maria knew it was unusual for a woman to write serious fiction, but that didn't stop her. The thought of producing something new in American literature gave Maria great pleasure. She decided to show Convers what she had written.

"But Maria did you really write this?" he asked. "Do you *mean* what you say, that it is entirely your own?"

Maria proudly told him she had written every word. Six weeks later, she completed her story. It was about an English woman who settles in New England and falls in love with an Indian man named Hobomok.

Like the heroines in Sir Walter Scott's novels, Maria's heroine was adventurous and brave. Maria also described the American Indians in her novel as truthfully as she could. Of course, whether the reading public would accept the kind of story Maria had written remained to be seen. In the 1800s, many people considered marriage between a white woman and an Indian man to be wrong.

Maria paid a publisher in Boston to print her book, titled *Hobomok*. It came out in May 1824. At the age of twenty-two, Maria had become the first author to publish a novel based on New England's history. Although her name did not appear on the book, word got out that the author was a young, unmarried woman. Some of Maria's friends warned her that she could no longer expect to be treated as a lady.

Not everyone disapproved of Maria's book. She heard that a man named George Ticknor had praised her writing. Mr. Ticknor was a Harvard professor and a friend of Convers's. He was also a leading figure in Boston's literary circle. Educated Bostonians came to his home to discuss the latest books and newest authors. One word from him could bring great success or failure to a writer. With Mr. Ticknor's support, Maria was sure more people would buy her book.

Maria decided to do something bold. In secret, she

wrote a letter to Mr. Ticknor in Boston. She asked the professor if he would help her promote her book. To Maria's delight, Mr. Ticknor immediately agreed to help. He asked a friend at a respected journal to write a favorable article about Maria's novel. And he continued to speak well of her work. As a result, *Hobomok* became a success, and Maria became a favorite in Boston's literary world.

Soon Maria was being invited to George Ticknor's home to meet other writers. People began to refer to her as "the brilliant Miss Francis." She was not sure she had lost her feminine charm, as so many women had predicted. She may not have been what people expected in a young lady, but she was well liked for her dignity, sympathy, and curiosity. Still, her success as an author did set her apart from other women.

While many women her age prepared for marriage, Maria continued to work on her writing. Sometimes she wondered if she was too well educated and outspoken. All she knew was that she could never be, or pretend to be, a helpless young lady. She would never be an ornament hanging on a gentleman's arm. No matter what happened, she had to be true to herself—even if that meant being on her own. Remaining independent and continuing to turn out books surely would not be such a terrible fate!

In early December, Maria attended a dinner party given by her brother and his wife. There she met a young man named David Lee Child. David had recently come to Watertown to study law with his uncle. He had a pleasant, open face and a deep, melodious voice. Maria's eyes never left his face as he talked.

David spoke dramatically about his years in Portugal as a representative of the United States. While living there, he had learned about a revolutionary war in Spain. The brave Spanish people had been using whatever weapons they could find to fight against an unjust king. David sympathized with the Spanish people so much that he quit his post and fought alongside them.

Maria was filled with admiration. Curious to learn more about David, she hoped to see him again. Several weeks later, Maria met David at another dinner party. That evening she wrote about him in her diary. "He is the most gallant man that has lived since the sixteenth century; and needs nothing but a helmet, shield, and chain of armour to make him a complete knight of chivalry."

Maria and David began to see each other often at dinner parties. They liked to tease each other and debate the latest issues. Behind the teasing, it was clear that they respected each other. But in less than a year, David left Watertown to live in Boston. He'd been given the chance to edit a new weekly paper, the *Massachusetts Journal.* If he had been thinking about marriage, he didn't say so. Maria said nothing either. She liked David very much, but she was in no hurry to marry anyone.

During David's absence, Maria continued to write. In December 1825, she published a second novel titled *The Rebels.* David published a good review of her book in his newspaper. "The brilliant Miss Francis" became more well-known than ever.

Along with her two novels, Maria had also published a book of stories for children titled *Evenings in New England.* She had wanted to show children as they really were—sometimes mischievous or naughty or mean, sometimes good. She felt that children just learning to read would enjoy such stories. And she wanted to encourage young readers to be kind and compassionate.

A Boston publisher took notice of her book. In the summer of 1826, Maria was offered the chance to edit a children's magazine. It would be the first magazine of its kind in the United States. At first Maria was reluctant to accept the offer. She felt that her true work lay in writing literature for adults. But the promise of a good salary led to her acceptance.

Maria's magazine, called *Juvenile Miscellany,* was an instant success. Children loved the cheerful stories, told simply and naturally, without preaching. The magazine also contained puzzles, poems, and crafts. One of Maria's poems was later made into a popular song about Thanksgiving, "Over the river and through the woods, to Grandmother's house we go."

Maria's life became very busy. Putting out the magazine took up only a portion of her time. She also taught school six hours a day and wrote short stories to maintain her literary reputation. Maria's evenings often included dinner parties, and her circle of admirers competed for her attention. She delighted in the turn her life had taken.

4

A Cry for Freedom

On an October night in 1827, Maria sat across from David Child as he talked about the advantages of married life. He had come to ask her to be his wife. Maria knew that she loved David. But she was not convinced that she wanted to marry anyone. She could see that David needed a woman's care. A button was missing from his coat, and his sleeves were frayed. But was she the woman to take care of him?

As they continued to talk, Maria began to know the answer. She had always been drawn to David because of his warm-hearted personality and his passionate defense of his beliefs. Even more important, Maria could see that he respected her own desires and goals. After four hours of talk, Maria agreed to marry him.

When Maria's father found out about his daughter's engagement, he was not pleased. David seemed like a dreamer. He may have been well educated, but could he take care of a wife? Mr. Francis worried that David was not careful with his money.

It was true. Whatever money David earned, he gave away or spent on his newspaper. But Maria wasn't worried. Surely her writing would bring in enough to help run their household. And besides, she had never let other people stop her from doing what she wanted. On October 19, 1828, Maria married David. At the age of twenty-six, she had become Lydia Maria Child.

The new couple set up housekeeping in a little house in Boston. Unlike many ladies, Maria did all her own cleaning, cooking, and washing. She also entertained visitors whenever they stopped by. Running a household was hard work, but she was careful to leave enough time each day for her writing.

Maria and David often talked about political issues of the day. Lately David had become upset by what was happening to the Cherokee Indians. A large number of Cherokees lived on fertile land in Georgia. White farmers wanted to use the land to grow crops, but the Cherokee Indians refused to give up what was theirs. Andrew Jackson said he would force the Indians to give up their land and move west.

Through his newspaper, David did what he could to gain support for the Cherokee people. What could Maria do? She thought long and hard. Then, while David wrote sitting on one side of a large desk, she began to write at the other side.

Drawing on her knowledge of American Indians, Maria wrote about the early histories of the Indian communities in New England. By January 1828, the stories were published as a book titled *The First Settlers of New England.* In it Maria argued that white people should not cause American Indians any more suffering. The early Americans, she said, had already treated the Indian people so unjustly. It was the first time Maria had spoken out on a political issue. But her book and David's newspaper articles were not enough to save the Cherokees. President Jackson forced the Indian people to move westward.

Maria enjoyed sharing her life and work with her husband. But David's generosity and carelessness became a source of anxiety for her. Seven months after their marriage, they were in debt and had to ask Maria's father for a loan. Maria realized that she needed to save some money. The *Juvenile Miscellany* continued to do well, but it wasn't enough.

Maria soon turned her attention to a new kind of writing. She guessed that many women had to run their households on small incomes. They would appreciate a book about saving money at home—a topic people rarely spoke about. Maria put down on paper all the little tricks and practical tips she felt a housewife should know. Besides recipes, the book contained information such as what cuts of meat to buy, how to set bread dough so that it would rise overnight, and how to make a good shampoo using rum.

When *The Frugal Housewife* came out in the fall of 1829, it became one of the most valued and popular books in American homes. No one in the United States had written anything like it. It sold six thousand copies the first year, and more after that. Many a housewife whose husband praised her housekeeping had Maria to thank for the compliments.

By this time, Maria had become famous throughout the United States. The *North American Review* wrote, "We are not sure that any woman in our country could outrank Mrs. Child. . . . Few female writers if any have done more or better things for our literature."

That summer a Boston printer named William Lloyd Garrison came to visit the Childs. Garrison had long admired Maria's writings and David's political essays. He wanted to start a new journal that would be devoted to the question of slavery, and he needed their help. David and Maria were familiar with Garrison. He was well known for his radical views on slavery. He had recently given a fiery speech in Boston in which he had pleaded for the freedom of the two million men and women doomed to a hopeless life of slavery.

Maria believed that slavery was wrong, and she was glad she lived in a state where black men and women could be free. But this man proposed the abolition of slavery in the South as well. He believed that all slaves should be set free immediately. David agreed with Garrison and promised to help him with his newspaper, the *Liberator.* But Maria was too independent to accept another person's beliefs right away. Still, Garrison had got her thinking. She felt compelled to learn more about slavery in the South.

For the next three years, she gathered information for a book about slavery. While preparing the book, Maria learned as much as she could about slavery in the South. In the process, she discovered how cruelly the slave traders treated African slaves. She read about how Africans were taken from their homeland and brought to the United States in terrible living conditions on overcrowded ships. The more she learned, the more she agreed with Garrison. Slavery was a terrible wrong and should be abolished.

In 1833 Maria published *An Appeal in Favor of That Class of Americans Called Africans.* The book called for an immediate end to slavery. Maria hoped to convince her readers of her message by describing the "miserable effects" of slavery. She also argued that Northerners treated free black people unfairly.

Black men and women were still second-class citizens. No hotel would give them a night's lodging. No restaurant would serve them a meal. At a theater, they had to sit in the gallery. At a church, they had to sit in the "Negro pew." And stagecoach drivers usually refused to let them ride with white passengers.

Maria knew her stand was unpopular, and reaction to her book came quickly. In the 1830s, few Americans agreed that slavery should be outlawed everywhere. The ideas about slavery in Maria's book made many people angry.

Maria had been considered the most popular woman writer in the country. But after the *Appeal* was published, Boston society closed its doors to her. There were no more invitations to dinner parties. Old friends crossed the street when they saw her coming.

What hurt Maria most was being shunned by Boston's literary circle. George Ticknor and other literary figures no longer welcomed her into their homes. People stopped buying her books. Even the *Juvenile Miscellany* suffered. In 1834 Maria was forced to give up her job as the magazine's editor. Too many mothers had canceled their subscriptions. They did not want their children to be influenced by someone who wrote about slavery as Maria did. Maria lost a lot when she spoke out against slavery.

But if she could change just one person's mind, she told herself, it would all be worth it.

Maria's book changed more than one person's mind. Her words had a powerful effect on many of her readers. A minister named William Ellery Channing came to see Maria after the *Appeal* came out. He confessed that the book had convinced him he could no longer remain silent on the issue of slavery. A lawyer named Wendell Phillips took up the cause and became a powerful speaker. And women who before had no interest in politics convinced their husbands to read the book. Almost overnight, Maria had become a powerful voice for freedom.

5

Letters from New York

After she published the *Appeal,* Maria continued to battle slavery. She had become part of a small group of Americans known as abolitionists. Through their speeches and writing, they began to touch the conscience of the nation. Many abolitionists in Northern cities formed branches of the American Anti-Slavery Society. David Child and William Lloyd Garrison were leaders of one in Boston. These societies sponsored antislavery speakers and raised money to buy slaves from their masters. They helped escaped slaves hide and travel north to places where they could live as free men and women.

The abolitionists' message made many people angry. Often antislavery pamphlets were stolen from post offices before they could be distributed. Southern states petitioned states in the North to make it a crime to print or distribute anything that might encourage slaves to revolt. Several times angry mobs tried to attack abolitionist speakers at public meetings. Once a mob stormed into Garrison's office, bent on violence. He was rescued just in time. Being an abolitionist could be dangerous. But none of this discouraged Maria.

Since the *Appeal* had come out, Maria was not earning very much from her other books. All the money she did earn seemed to end up being used for David's newspaper, the *Massachusetts Journal*. As a result, the Childs plunged even deeper into debt. To their relief, a way out presented itself. In 1835 they were offered positions in England as agents for the Anti-Slavery Society. The Anti-Slavery Society wanted the Childs to raise support and money from people in England to help end slavery. They promised to pay the Childs a salary for their work.

David and Maria jumped at the chance to leave their debts behind. They could spread the abolitionists' message overseas. And Maria could promote her books in England, where they had been selling well.

That summer the two traveled to New York to meet the ship that would take them to England. Their departure was set for August 16, and they met their ship on that day. But just before the ship departed, David was arrested. He and Maria learned that they could not leave for England with David's large debts still unpaid. They were forced to return home.

A heavy-hearted Maria hoped they could still find a way to go to England, but David soon had another plan. Like many abolitionists, he and Maria did not want to buy products, such as sugar, that had been produced by slaves. They believed that if enough people stopped buying slave-labor goods, Southerners would stop using slaves. David suggested that he should go to France, where farmers had discovered how to make sugar from a kind of beet. He could learn about the French process and start a sugar beet farm in America—without using slaves.

Maria would miss David if he went to France without her, but she believed in his plans. David's idea was presented to the Anti-Slavery Society, and money was found to send him to Europe. He left for France in October 1836. In the meantime, Maria moved in with her father in a small town outside of Boston.

While David was away, Maria worked with other women in the abolitionist movement. In May 1837, Maria was asked to represent the Boston Female Anti-Slavery Society at the Anti-Slavery Convention of American Women in New York. Here Maria heard two outspoken sisters from South Carolina.

Sarah and Angelina Grimké made people very angry—not only because of what they said but because they spoke out in public. It was considered highly improper for women to make speeches about anything. Maria didn't agree with all of their ideas, but she was glad to hear other women speak out against slavery.

In the fall of 1837, David returned to the United States after more than a year in France. He set out to buy farmland on which he could try growing sugar beets. Maria's father agreed to help pay for the farm and equipment if he could live with Maria and David. With Mr. Francis's help, David and Maria purchased a farm in Northampton, one hundred miles from Boston. Maria found herself keeping house for her husband, her father, and two hired men. She cooked, washed, sewed quilts, mended the men's clothing, and cared for two horses, one cow, and two oxen.

Maria's father proved to be difficult to live with. There were continual requests: Mr. Francis's coat needed mending. Would Maria put a patch on the elbow? It was too cold in the house. Would Maria lay a fire in the fireplace? An exhausted Maria wrote to a friend that it was almost too much to bear.

Life in Northampton did not seem to suit Mr. Francis. After several months, he left the farm. Maria and David had counted on his help to pay off the debts that had mounted when they started farming. Without his help, Maria would have to find a way to earn extra money while David ran the farm.

The answer to their problems came in the form of a letter from William Lloyd Garrison. The abolitionist newspaper the *National Anti-Slavery Standard* needed help. Would David and Maria come to New York and edit it? Maria knew that David couldn't give up the farm after all the beet experiments he had done. But the money would be helpful. They had been promised a yearly salary of one thousand dollars to edit the paper. David persuaded Maria to go to New York by herself. He told her she was the perfect person for that position, even though it meant another separation for them. He promised to write her often and visit whenever he could.

In a way, Maria was ready to leave Northampton. She was becoming more upset with David. His constant trouble with debts prevented her from focusing her energies on her writing. And she would be able to live in an exciting city, working for a newspaper she believed in. But as much as she looked forward to her newspaper work, she was also afraid of loneliness. Who would tease her when she felt low, like David did? Who would watch over him to see that he did not catch cold? Before she left for New York, she knitted socks for him, sewed all his buttons on tightly, and laid out candles in case the lamp oil gave out.

When Maria arrived in New York in May 1841, she discovered that she was the entire staff of the *Standard*. She was expected to put out a four-page paper each week. Although she had been promised one thousand dollars a year, there was little money to pay her. In spite of this, Maria did her best to make the paper interesting. As a woman, she knew that many eyes were upon her, judging her work. She was determined not to fail. She set about to make the *Standard* a "family newspaper" by adding features that would appeal to many readers. She did not want only abolitionists to read the paper. Maria hoped to convert new people to the cause by making the paper more interesting to more people.

Maria filled the newspaper's pages with household advice, short stories, cartoons, and poetry. To do this, she read many current books and magazines. She also read other leading newspapers and attended meetings that were expected to make news. Then she wrote articles about the most current events. Often she was too tired at the end of the day to do her washing, ironing, and mending.

Her hard work soon paid off. Sales of the newspaper increased to four thousand copies each week.

Much of the newspaper's popularity was due to Maria's column "Letters from New York." To write these "letters," Maria explored parts of the city that ordinary people might never see. She wrote about the pigs that rooted around in many gutters. She visited shipyards and wrote about the graceful steamships being built. She wrote about P. T. Barnum's museum, where he exhibited two-headed cows and other unusual creatures. And she described the work of young artists whose paintings she admired at the American Art Union. She even traveled up the Hudson River to visit Sing Sing Prison. Her vivid descriptions of the prisoners' lives made readers aware of how badly the prisoners were treated.

Maria's paper pleased some abolitionists. But others did not approve of her work. Maria found herself caught in the middle. By 1842 the American Anti-Slavery Society had begun to splinter into different groups. Some abolitionists believed they should continue putting pressure on politicians to change the laws. Others felt the time had come to take more direct action. Some even urged breaking up the nation into separate countries.

Maria had been criticized for being overly cautious with the newspaper. Some abolitionists said that the newspaper should have a stronger antislavery message. They did not want the paper to appeal to more people if it meant watering down that message. Maria did not agree. She refused to change the paper to suit someone else's opinion. Instead, she felt she had no choice but to quit her job as editor.

When Maria left the *Standard* in May 1843, she felt a mixture of sadness and relief. In her view, abolitionists had become too busy fighting with each other to be successful in their fight for freedom. She decided to cut her ties to the Anti-Slavery Society after nearly ten years of involvement.

During this time, David decided to sell the farm in Northampton. The sugar beet experiments had not been successful, and he was still in debt. Without money from Maria's work on the *Standard,* they had no income. Would David send them deeper into debt? Maria decided to take stock of her life.

Although she loved David, she could no longer watch all her hard-earned money go toward his debts. She decided to remove her money from David's name, so it would be safe from his creditors. She would also remain in New York and write serious literature—something she had all but given up. While David looked for work, she could maintain her independent life in the city. At the age of forty-one, Maria looked forward to the future.

6

A House Divided

During the next seven years, Maria published three volumes of children's stories, several books and stories for adults, and a collection of her "Letters from New York." She became a celebrity once again.

Whenever David visited Maria, she was happy to see him. It was true that she had to spend the days of his visit washing and mending his clothes. Yet without him, she was dreadfully lonely. By 1850 they decided to find a home together. Not being able to afford lodging for two in New York, they moved to a farm outside Boston. Then, three years later, they moved to Wayland, Massachusetts, where Maria's father was living. Old Mr. Francis's health had been declining, and he needed someone to care for him.

In Wayland David carried on a small law practice, grew beans and squash, and looked after the fruit trees on their lot. Maria planted tulips and daffodils to add color to their yard. When the demands of the two men got to be too much, she retreated to a pond over the hill. There she could smell the apples in the orchard and listen to the wrens and red-winged blackbirds among the cattails.

During all this time, Maria had stayed away from politics. She kept up-to-date on the slavery question, but she did not want to get involved personally. Violent events in the nation changed her mind.

In the 1850s, settlers in western territories such as Kansas could not agree on how to deal with slavery. Some people wanted these territories to allow slavery. Others believed that slavery should be outlawed in the West. By 1856 Kansas had become a bloody battleground between settlers who were for and against slavery. Battles even erupted in Congress. Senator Charles Sumner of Massachusetts made a speech attacking the proslavery settlers in Kansas. Afterward he was beaten by a South Carolina congressman wielding a cane. News of the attack horrified Maria. Mr. Sumner had read Maria's antislavery writings, and Maria had followed his work in Congress.

Maria felt she had to do something. Taking up her pen, she began to write a story to inspire the divided abolitionist groups. She called her story "The Kansas Emigrants." Her characters were crusaders who fought to keep the territory of Kansas free of slavery. In October and November 1856, the *New York Tribune* printed her story. Thousands of people read it. Once again Maria had become a voice for freedom.

Maria's story came out during a heated presidential campaign between John C. Frémont and James Buchanan. Frémont had been nominated by the newly organized Republican Party. He stood for the right of Congress to vote against slavery in the western territories.

Maria believed that Frémont might prevent the country from splitting apart and going to war. "If the Slave-Power is checked *now,* it will *never* regain its strength," she wrote to a friend. "If it is *not* checked, civil war is inevitable."

Maria did everything she could to get Frémont elected. The only thing she couldn't do was cast her own ballot. As a woman, Maria did not have the right to vote. She was disappointed when James Buchanan won the election.

Shortly after the election, Maria's father became very ill. On Thanksgiving Day, Mr. Francis died in Wayland with Maria at his side. In his will, he left Maria and David his house and some wooded land. They decided to stay in Wayland. They were happy with their simple rural style of living, and Maria contented herself with occasional visits to friends in Boston.

As Maria's life fell into a peaceful routine, the country seemed to become more and more divided. A young lawyer named Abraham Lincoln was running in Illinois for the U.S. Senate. He expressed what many others had said in the past: "A house divided against itself cannot stand." The country could not survive if half of it wanted slavery while the other half wanted freedom.

While arguments raged throughout the land, one man decided to take the law into his own hands. On October 16, 1859, John Brown invaded the town of Harpers Ferry in Virginia with a small group of men. He hoped to bring about a widespread revolt among the slaves. His plan failed, and he was captured and put on trial as a traitor.

To Maria, John Brown's action was too extreme,

but she couldn't help admiring him. While John Brown waited in a Virginia prison for his trial, Maria wrote to him. She also wrote to Governor Wise of Virginia. In her letter, she asked for permission to visit Brown.

The governor responded to Maria's request with a polite but angry letter. It was people like her who had led John Brown to attack Harpers Ferry, he said. Therefore Maria and other abolitionists were partly to blame for the result.

The governor's letter outraged Maria, and she responded with an angry letter of her own. In her second letter she argued that it was the slave owners who were responsible for John Brown's actions. *They* had been the ones to treat slaves so poorly. John Brown had merely tried to help black men and women gain their freedom.

These letters found their way onto the pages of several newspapers. Maria's mailbox filled up with angry letters from the South. Some letter-writers said they would no longer read her works. That had never stopped Maria from speaking out before. If anything, the letters prompted her to further action. She wrote pamphlets against slavery and mailed hundreds of them to politicians. Her energy drove her from task to task.

In the summer of 1860, Maria received a request from a former slave named Harriet Jacobs. Harriet had written a story about her years in slavery and her escape to freedom. She wondered if Maria might edit it and help get it published.

Harriet's book came out in 1861 under the title *Incidents in the Life of a Slave Girl.* Maria hoped Harriet's story would show readers that slavery must be stopped, especially since the country's new president did not plan on outlawing it in the South.

Abraham Lincoln had won the presidential election in November 1860. He announced that he would not interfere with slavery where it was already practiced. But if the Southern states wanted war, then the North was ready to fight. Five weeks after Lincoln took office in the spring of 1861, Southern soldiers attacked Fort Sumter, and the Civil War began.

Maria sank into a depression when she heard Northern leaders talk about the war. They said that the Union was fighting to put down treason. Their purpose was not to meddle with slavery. As much as she hated war, Maria hoped it would not end until slavery was completely overthrown.

7

More Work to Be Done

On New Year's Day, 1863, Maria's wish came true. On that day, President Lincoln issued the Emancipation Proclamation. Like many Americans, Lincoln had come to believe that the Civil War should not end until slavery was abolished. The president's official proclamation declared that slaves should be free in the rebelling states. But it was not until the end of the war, when the South surrendered in April 1865, that Congress passed the Thirteenth Amendment to the Constitution. With this amendment, the slaves were truly freed. What Maria had worked for, for thirty-five years, had finally happened.

Maria rejoiced at the news, but much work remained to be done. It had been against the law in the South to teach slaves how to read or write. Most had never been allowed to study in schools or learn about their own history. And in many states, freed slaves continued to receive unfair treatment. The people who had created antislavery societies began to set up freedmen's societies after the war. They opened schools for freed slaves, raised money, and wrote letters to congressmen. Maria wanted to help.

In 1865 she gathered material for a new book, *The Freedman's Book*. She filled it with practical advice— how to run a household, how to care for animals, how to take care of one's health. She also included stories and poems by black men and women, and short biographies of black heroes. Maria wanted to educate freed slaves and give them hope. She wanted to show them what other black men and women had "accomplished, under great disadvantages."

Publishers refused to print *The Freedman's Book* unless Maria paid a share of the cost. Somehow she raised six hundred dollars and sent off her only copy. She hoped the book would be bought and used by freed slaves in the South.

It turned out that few freed slaves could afford to buy any books at all. So Maria bought up copies of *The Freedman's Book* herself and gave them away through the Freedman's Aid Society.

During this time, Maria also wrote letters to newspapers, congressmen, and magazine editors. She asked them to help protect the rights of the freedmen. She also argued that black men should have the right to vote alongside white men. Not being able to vote herself still made Maria angry. But she felt that giving black men the right to vote was just as important as giving women that right.

Maria and David lived on whatever her writing brought in. If anything was left over, it was sent away to help the freedmen. With so much work to be done, Maria neglected her appearance. Never interested in fashion, she continued to wear her worn-out clothes. To Maria, there were more important places for her money than new clothes.

In the last years of her life, Maria continued to fight for people's rights: women's right to vote, the right to better living conditions for American Indians, and equal rights for new immigrants to the United States. For as long as she lived, letters and articles flowed in a steady stream from her pen.

Maria died on October 20, 1880, at the age of

seventy-eight. She had proved that a woman could be a powerful voice in a man's world. At her funeral, Maria's friend Wendell Phillips said of her, "She was ready to die for a principle and starve for an idea." She was, indeed, the conscience of a nation.

Bibliography

Baer, Helene. *The Heart Is Like Heaven.* Philadelphia: University of Pennsylvania Press, 1964.

Child, Lydia Maria. *An Appeal in Favor of That Class of Americans Called Africans.* 1836. Reprint, New York: Arno Press, 1968.

Child, L. Maria. *The Freedman's Book.* 1865. Reprint, New York: Arno Press, 1968.

Child, L. Maria. *Letters of Lydia Maria Child.* Boston: Houghton, Mifflin and Co., 1883.

Clifford, Deborah Pickman. *Crusader for Freedom: A Life of Lydia Maria Child.* Boston: Beacon Press, 1992.

Karcher, Carolyn L. *The First Woman in the Republic: A Cultural Biography of Lydia Maria Child.* Durham, NC: Duke University Press, 1994.

Karcher, Carolyn L., editor. *Hobomok & Other Writings on Indians.* New Brunswick, NJ: Rutgers University Press, 1986.

Meltzer, Milton. *Tongue of Flame: The Life of Lydia Maria Child.* New York: Crowell, 1965.

Meltzer, Milton and Patricia G. Holland, editors. *Lydia Maria Child: Selected Letters, 1817–1880.* Amherst, MA: University of Massachusetts Press, 1982.

Index

About the Author

Erica Stux spent most of her life in Ohio, growing up in Cincinnati and then living in Akron. She received a B.A. and M.A. in chemistry at the University of Cincinnati and worked for several years as a chemist. After she had children of her own, Erica began writing and publishing books for young people. She also enjoys songwriting, bird watching, and playing bridge. Erica currently lives in Chatsworth, California, near Los Angeles.

About the Illustrator

Mary O'Keefe Young studied art at Parsons School of Design in New York City and has illustrated 17 books for children. In addition to illustration, Mary enjoys photography, sewing costumes, and painting portraits. Raised in Larchmont, New York, she now has her studio in nearby White Plains. Mary is also the illustrator of *The Snow Walker, Fire at the Triangle Factory, The Road to Seneca Falls: A Story About Elizabeth Cady Stanton,* and *Revolutionary Poet: A Story about Phillis Wheatley,* all published by Carolrhoda Books.